MW01593490

CONTENTS

FOREWORD

Our Lord and Savior, Jesus Christ, commanded His church to go into all the world and preach the Gospel to every creature. This mandate of evangelism necessitates our taking the Gospel to that group known as Jehovah's Witnesses.

Yet many Christians hesitate to face one of this cult in a witness situation for one of two reasons. First, the Christian who would face a Jehovah's Witness must know his own doctrine, plus the convictions of the Witnesses, which few Christians do.

Second, though the Jehovah's Witnesses are wrong in their beliefs, they are extremely knowledgeable of Scripture and the arguments from the Bible which they think support their position. The one facing them in a witnessing confrontation must know the Scriptures, especially those refuting the Witnesses' beliefs and arguments which, again, few Christians do.

Dr. Pat Campbell, writing from the experience of a converted Jehovah's Witness, does the evangelical world of our day a great service by solving both of these problems for us. In the unfolding of this work, he gives us both a summary of the Witness doctrine, and of Christian doctrine, and also presents us with a clear method to evangelize the Jehovah's Witness zealot.

This book can be used by an individual Christian for his personal benefit for evangelism or it could be the basis of a group study of the way to evangelize Jehovah's Witnesses. May our God of grace use it in either of these ways and ultimately to the reaching of souls for our Lord Jesus Christ.

Dr. Richard P. Belcher, Professor
Columbia Bible College
Columbia, South Carolina

How To
Share
Christ
With A
Jehovah's Witness

third edition

ISBN 1-931600-46-5

Printed in the United States of America

PREFACE

It was in the eighth grade that I was introduced to the teachings of the Jehovah's Witnesses by my Aunt Audrey and I remained committed to their doctrines until my conversion to Christ in my freshman year of college in January, 1964.

My brother-in-law's father, Rev. Charles Taylor, and Rev. Bill Davis, both Southern Baptist preachers, were used of God to lead me to the saving knowledge of Christ.

Having come out of the Jehovah's Witnesses, God has directed me concerning a method to share the Gospel of Jesus Christ with them.

This is not the only way, but a definite plan to witness to them. I have personally found this approach to be very helpful in sharing Christ with them.

It is my prayer that God would use this booklet to help you win Jehovah's Witnesses to the saving grace and knowledge of Jesus Christ our Lord.

Pat Campbell

CHAPTER ONE

A Brief History of the Jehovah's Witnesses

The Jehovah's Witnesses, who are officially known as the Watchtower Bible and Tract Society, have their origins in the person and work of Charles Taze Russell. He was born on February 16, 1852, near Pittsburgh, Pennsylvania. In 1870, at the age of 18, he organized a Bible class in Pittsburgh in which he was finally elected in 1876 the "Pastor" of the group. In 1879 he founded the magazine called Zion's Watchtower in which he published his own interpretations of the Bible, and finally, in 1886, published his first of seven books now entitled Studies in the Scriptures.

Russell's life was surrounded with scandal and frequent clashes with the courts. He perjured himself in court and in 1906 his wife was granted a divorce by the Judge of the High Court of Ontario who stated that no woman should have to live with such an egotistical and arrogant man. He was charged by The Brooklyn Eagle with the practice of fraud and he was known to induce sick people to turn over their fortunes to his organizations. He continued his teachings until his death on October 31, 1916 aboard a transcontinental train in Texas. It is reported that by the time of his death in 1916 that

"Pastor" Russell, according to the Watchtower, traveled more than a million miles, gave more than thirty-thousand sermons and wrote books totalling over fifty thousand pages. (Understanding the Cults, Here's Life Publishers, 1962, p. 55).

Following Russell's death, the Society's legal counselor, Joseph Franklin Rutherford, was unanimously chosen to be the second President of the Watchtower Bible and Tract Society on January 6, 1917. Rutherford was extremely vocal and aggressive in attacking the doctrines of "organized religion" through his radio talks, phonograph recordings, and numerous books, which continued until his death on January 8, 1942 from cancer at his mansion, "Beth Sarim," in San Diego, California. He died at 72, but not without leaving his strong influence upon the Watchtower Society.

Walter Martin says that Russell was a literary pygmy compared to Rutherford. He states, "The prolific Judge wrote over one hundred books and pamphlets, and his works as of 1941 had been translated into eighty languages." (The Kingdom of the Cults, Bethany, 1965, p. 48.). Rutherford was the one responsible for the name "Jehovah's Witnesses" which was adopted on October 9, 1931 at the Annual Convention in Columbus, Ohio.

Following the death of Rutherford, Nathan Homer Knorr was elected President of the "Jehovah's Witnesses." Under his leadership, the organization increased from 115,000 to over two million members. He was responsible for the Gilead Missionary Training School in South Lansing, New York, and in 1961 under his leadership, the Society produced its own English translation of the Bible entitled The New World Translation of Holy Scriptures. It was also during Knorr's administration that the endless books and booklets appeared under the copyright of the Watchtower Bible and Tract Society without bearing the name of individual authors. A "committee" now handles the mass of printed matter that leaves the printing press.

Knorr followed in the footsteps of Russell and Rutherford and continued the hostile attacks on Christianity. He died in June of 1977, and Frederick W. Franz, a long time leader and, at that time, Vice-President of the Society, was elected President and continues to give leadership to the Society similar to his predecessors. The Jehovah's Witnesses continue to grow in spite of periodic setbacks due to the failure of their date setting for the end of the world, which they refer to as the battle of Armageddon, in which all of Christendom shall be destroyed.

This brief history is given to provide the reader a thumbnail sketch of the "Jehovah's Witnesses" background to show first of all its recent history, and second, to acquaint the reader with the key men at the leadership helm of the Society. We will now look at the doctrinal position of the Jehovah's Witnesses followed by some guidelines that are very helpful to remember when one is witnessing to a Jehovah's Witness.

CHAPTER TWO

The Doctrinal Position of the Jehovah's Witnesses

The following twelve articles represent the essential doctrines upon which the Jehovah's Witnesses build their organization.

I.   God is a solitary being who has existed from all eternity and created everything that exists, both visible and invisible. There is no Trinity.

II.   Jesus Christ is the beginning of God's creation. He is not the eternal Son of God but was created by God as the Word and was the active agent in the creation of all other things. He is also known as Michael the Archangel. He is 'a god' but not the Almighty God Jehovah. Jesus is the Son of God but not God Himself. He became the man Jesus, who was fully human, but not divine. He suffered on a torture stake as a ransom for man's sin.

III. The Holy Spirit is not a person but God's active force in the world. The Holy Spirit is the invisible active force of Jehovah God that moves his servants to do his will. The Holy Spirit is neither divine nor the third person of the Trinity.

IV.   The Bible is God's Word and is fully inspired and true in everything that it teaches. The Bible has been preserved by Jehovah to reveal His purposes to His followers.

V.   Satan is a great angel who rebelled against God and persuaded a group of angels or demons to follow him in this act. Satan tempted man so that sin and death came upon mankind. Satan and his angels will be annihilated forever.

VI.   Man was created by Jehovah God after His image. He willfully chose to sin and therefore all men are born sinners. Those who are obedient to Jehovah and follow Jesus Christ faithfully unto death will inherit the heavenly Kingdom and rule with Christ. These are the 144,000 called the 'annointed class' or 'little flock'. The rest of the Jehovah's Witnesses, called the great crowd, will inherit a new earth where they will live forever. All who reject Jehovah will be destroyed forever.

VII. Man does not have an immortal soul; therefore, he does not exist forever. At death man is nonexistent but all the Jehovah's Witnesses of the great crowd will be physically resurrected to live on the new earth. These are the ones whom Jehovah has in His memory.

VIII. There is no such place as an eternal hell of fire and brimstone. Hell is only the common grave of mankind. Eternal punishment does not mean "eternal torment" of living souls, but is an eternal annihilation.

IX. The atonement for our sins was a ransom paid by Jesus Christ to Jehovah God. It removed the effects of Adam's sin and all his offspring and became the basis for the new world of right-eousness. The payment was Christ's physical body; therefore it could not be raised from the dead. Thus, the man Jesus is forever dead and He was resurrected a spirit person.

X. Jesus Christ returned to the earth as an invis-ible spirit in 1914 to take His kingdom power and reign invisibly until the Battle of Armaged-don when all Christendom shall be destroyed. After Armageddon, Christ will set up his 1,000 year reign upon the earth.

XI. Jehovah's kingdom is supreme. It is separate from human government which is Satan's vis-ible organization. There can be no allegiance to any human government but to Jehovah God only.

XII. God's visible organization on the earth today which receives His theocratic guidance and di-rection is the Jehovah's Witnesses with its headquarters in Brooklyn, New York. There is a governing body of older men made up of "the faithful and discreet slave," and they guide the organization. (The Kingdom of the Cults, Be-thany, 1965, pp. 51-52) and (You Can Live For-ever In Paradise on Earth, 1982, pp. 7-255.)

CHAPTER THREE

Six Guidelines to Remember When Witnessing to a Jehovah's Witness

1. **It is imperative that those who are going to witness to a Jehovah's Witness must be well-grounded and firmly secure in their knowledge of Christianity.**

    Because of their training and indoctrination, Jehovah's Witnesses can disconcert and emotionally disturb the unprepared and doctrinally shallow believer. Only the mature and those deeply rooted in Scripture are prepared to confront a Jehovah's Witness. Be certain that you are spiritually and Scripturally ready to share your faith with a Jehovah's Witness. You must heed the admonition of the Apostle Peter in I Peter 3:15, "but sanctify Christ as Lord in your hearts, always being ready to make a defense to everyone who asks you to give an account for the hope that is in you, yet with gentleness and reverence."

2. **Do not discuss subjects like: Why they don't salute the flag. Why they don't give blood. Why they don't celebrate Christ-**

mas, etc., etc.

The discussion of these subjects will never accomplish the purpose of winning Jehovah's Witnesses to Jesus Christ. To discuss these subjects is to major on the minor issue rather than the primary one. It is to generate a lot of heat and energy but to accomplish little. Only when we focus upon the foundational doctrines of Christ's person, the Trinity, the resurrection, salvation, etc., can we hope to win them to Christ. Don't get sidetracked by discussing secondary issues that don't deal with the heart of the matter.

3.   **Discuss only the main doctrinal subjects such as the Deity of Christ, the personality of the Holy Spirit, the triune nature of God, the bodily resurrection of Christ, etc.**

This booklet will contain a structure for you to follow concerning these main issues. It is best to stay on one subject, such as the Deity of Christ and exhaust it before moving or jumping to another subject. When Jehovah's Witnesses try to move to another subject before the one you are discussing has been exhausted, bring them back to the subject.

4.   **Always read the full context of Scripture and then point out the "key verse" and ask them what they think it means. After they give their explanation, then you can give them the biblical understanding of the text in context.**

For example, if you are quoting from Luke's Gospel concerning the resurrection of Christ from

Chapter 24:36-43, read all of these verses and then ask them what verse 39 means. After they give their answer, then share with them that Christ is proving to the disciples that He is not just a spirit [Jehovah's Witnesses believe that He was just a spirit after the resurrection], but a physical resurrection. The key verse is 39, "See my hands and my feet, that it is I myself; touch me and see, for a spirit does not have flesh and bones as you see that I have." Jesus was proving to the disciples He was not just a spirit but a real tangible physical resurrected body. "And when He had said this, He showed them His hands and His feet." (vs. 40).

5.   Don't expect an instant conversion the first time you witness to them. Their minds have been "programmed" to think in a certain way and they are spiritually blind to the truth of God's Word. Maintain the initiative with them and clearly define your terms.

Rarely are Jehovah's Witnesses converted to Christ with one encounter. Because of the power of Satan upon their lives, it will take several, if not many periods of discussion with them. All cults are brainwashed to think in a certain pattern and this is one of the main reasons they cannot receive the truth. But when we maintain the initiative in our witness to them and clearly and precisely define our terms, God can use this approach to break down their defenses and blindness. But remember that they can be won to the saving knowledge of Christ but it will take much time, patience, work and diligent prayer. The next principle is strategic.

6.   Always remember that the Holy Spirit will use the truth of God's Word to penetrate into their hearts and bring conviction of their lostness. Always share your personal testimony with them.

No matter how blind a person may be to the truth of God's Word, we have assurance that God's Holy Spirit is present and at work upon the hearts and minds of those hearing the true Gospel. John's Gospel, Chapter 16, says that the Holy Spirit would convict the world concerning sin, and righteousness, and judgment (vs. 8). As we present the truth of God's Word to Jehovah's Witnesses, the Holy Spirit of God is the one who can convict, draw and illuminate their hearts and minds to the reality of Jesus Christ. Every Christian can have a bold confidence that God's Spirit is at work in the witnessing encounter with Jehovah's Witnesses. He is able to penetrate their spiritual darkness and reveal the light of the glorious Gospel of Jesus Christ. Let not the Christian despair.

Your personal testimony of how Christ saved you can have a powerful impact upon Jehovah's Witnesses and can be used of God to help win them to Christ. Learn to share your testimony in a three to five minute period using the following outline:

1. My life before I received Christ.
2. How I received Christ.
3. What my life has been since I received Christ.

Be diligent in your prayer and study and trust God's Spirit to guide and direct you in each encounter with them. Only with the patience of Job can you be effective in winning Jehovah's Witnesses to the Lord. But the results of winning them to Christ are worth all the effort and energy expended toward this purpose.

CHAPTER FOUR

A Skeletal Outline and Explanation of Witnessing to a Jehovah's Witness

The following is a skeletal outline and explanation with the five best Scriptural references to use when witnessing to a Jehovah's Witness.

1. Jesus Christ

You must show them Scripturally that Jesus Christ is the eternal, only begotten Son of God and not the first created angel called Michael the Archangel.

Scripture	Key Verses
John 1:1-18 .... vs.	1, 14, 18
John 8:48-59 .... vs.	58
John 20:26-29 .... vs.	28
Titus 2:11-14 .... vs.	13
Hebrews 1:1-14 .... vs.	4-6, 13-14

2. The Holy Spirit

You must show them Scripturally that the Holy

Spirit is a person and that He is God and not just God's active impersonal force and power.

Scripture   Key Verses

John 14:16-26 .... vs. 26
John 15:18-27 .... vs. 26
John 16:1-15 .... vs. 14
Acts 13:1-3 .... vs. 2
Romans 8:1-27 .... vs. 13-16, 26-27

3. The Trinity

You must show them Scripturally that there is one God in three persons: The Father, the Son, the Holy Spirit and that all three persons are God and not just one God in one person called Jehovah.

Scripture   Key Verses

Matthew 3:13-17 .... vs. 16-17
Matthew 28:16-20 .... vs. 19
Romans 8:26-39 .... vs. 27, 31, 34
Ephesians 1:3-14 .... vs. 3, 7, 13
I Peter 1:1-2 .... vs. 2

4. The Resurrection

You must show them Scripturally that Jesus Christ was raised from the dead with the same physical body He had before His crucifixion but that His body was raised incorruptible and glorified and so He is not just a spirit creature.

Scripture   Key Verses

Matthew 28:1-20 .... vs. 6, 9
Luke 24:36-49 .... vs. 37, 39-40,46
John 2:13-22 .... vs. 19-22
Acts 13:15-41 .... vs. 30, 33-34,37
I Corinthians 15:1-58.............. vs. 4, 12-28

5. Salvation

You must show them Scripturally that we are
saved by pure grace through repentance toward
God and faith in the Lord Jesus Christ and not
on the basis of any human merit or good works
of any kind.

Scripture   Key Verses

John 1:9-13 .... vs. 12
Acts 20:17-35 .... vs. 21
Romans 4:1-16 .... vs. 3, 5, 16
Ephesians 2:1-10 .... vs. 8-9
Titus 3:1-7 .... vs. 5

6. Heaven

You must show them Scripturally that everyone
who is a Christian has the hope of going to
heaven and not just 144,000 Jehovah's Witnesses.

Scripture   Key Verses

John 14:1-6 .... vs. 2-3
II Corinthians 5:1-10 .... vs. 1-2, 8
Philippians 3:17-21 .... vs. 20-21

I Thessalonians 4:13-18 .... vs. 16-18
Revelation 21:10-27 .... vs. 10, 22-27

7. Hell

You must show them Scripturally that hell is a real place of conscious eternal torment for the lost sinner and not just the grave where a person totally ceases to exist.

Scripture	Key Verses
Matthew 10:24-33 .... vs.	28
Matthew 25:31-46 .... vs.	41, 46
Luke 16:19-31 .... vs.	22-25
Revelation 14:9-12 .... vs.	10-11
Revelation 20:11-15 .... vs.	14-15

8. The Second Coming of Jesus Christ

You must show them Scripturally that Jesus Christ will return visibly, bodily, and in glory with His angels to gather together His church, destroy the Antichrist and his evil government at the battle of Armageddon and reign as King of Kings and Lord of Lords; and not that He returned invisibly in 1914 to rule His Kingdom until the battle of Armageddon which will destroy everyone but the Jehovah's Witnesses.

Scripture	Key Verses
Matthew 24:1-31 .... vs.	29-31
I Thessalonians 4:13-18 .... vs.	16-18
II Thessalonians 2:1-12 .... vs.	3, 8
Revelation 19:11-21 .... vs.	11, 19-21
Revelation 20:1-10 .... vs.	2, 4-10

CHAPTER FIVE

An Expanded Version and Explanation of Witnessing to a Jehovah's Witness

The following material is an expanded version of the skeletal outline. It is best to start with the doctrine of Christ and determine to stay on that subject until it has been exhausted, and then move on to the next subject. They will constantly try to get you away from the doctrinal subject you are discussing but you <u>must</u> not allow yourself to become sidetracked on another subject. Keep bringing them back to the subject you are discussing until you have treated it thoroughly and then move to the next doctrine. You must learn to communicate clearly the doctrinal position of Christianity and the key verses for each subject.

I.   JESUS CHRIST

You must show them Scripturally that Jesus Christ is the eternal, only begotten Son of God and not the first created angel called Michael the Archangel.

The Jehovah's Witnesses' Teaching Concerning Jesus Christ

Jehovah's Witnesses teach concerning Christ that:

". . . the true Scriptures speak of God's Son, the Word as 'a god.' He is a 'mighty god,' but not the Almighty God, who is Jehovah" (The Truth Shall Make You Free, Brooklyn: Watchtower Bible and Tract Society, 1943, p. 47).

". . . Jesus was 'the Son of God.' Not God himself!" ("The Word" Who Is He?, p. 20).

In other words, he was the first and direct creation of Jehovah God (The Kingdom Is At Hand, Brooklyn: Watchtower Bible and Tract Society, 1944, pp. 46, 47, 49).

They teach that Christ had a beginning, and that He was created by God, and that He was Michael the Archangel. They do not believe that He is the eternal Son of God.

Evangelical Christianity's Teaching Concerning Jesus Christ

Evangelical Christianity believes and teaches that Jesus Christ is the eternal Son of God, the second person of the Trinity, who became the God-man through His supernatural birth in the virgin Mary. He is truly God, and truly man.

One Person (The Lord Jesus Christ)
In 2 Natures (Deity and Humanity)

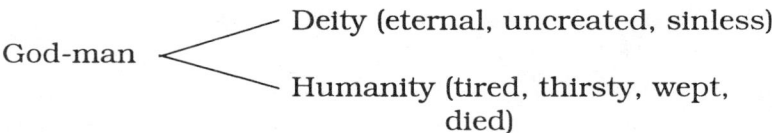

God-man — Deity (eternal, uncreated, sinless)

Humanity (tired, thirsty, wept, died)

The Greek word for only begotten (monogenas) means: unique in kind, the one and only. Thus, Jesus Christ is the unique, one and only begotten Son of God (John 3:16).

Scriptures to Use
Concerning Jesus Christ

The following Scriptures need to be learned and quoted when witnessing to Jehovah's Witnesses concerning Jesus Christ.

Scripture	Key Verses
Isaiah 44:1-8	vs. 6
Matthew 11:25-30	vs. 27
Matthew 14:22-36	vs. 33
Matthew 16:13-20	vs. 15-16
Mark 2:1-12	vs. 10-11
Luke 22:66-71	vs. 70
John 1:1-18	vs. 1, 14, 18
John 5:1-18	vs. 18
John 8:48-59	vs. 58
John 10:22-39	vs. 30
John 11:1-44	vs. 25-27
John 17:1-5	vs. 5
John 20:26-31	vs. 28, 30-31
Romans 9:1-5	vs. 5
Philippians 2:5-11	vs. 11
Colossians 1:15-23	vs. 16
Colossians 2:8-15	vs. 9

Concerning the word firstborn in Colossians 1:15, you need to know that the Greek word (proto-tokos) means prime source, having first place. It does not mean first created, as the Jehovah's Witnesses try to use it. The following two translations capture the true meaning of the word.

His firstborn son who existed before any created thing.
The Williams Translation

His is the primacy over all created things.
The New English Bible

II.   THE HOLY SPIRIT

You must show them Scripturally that the Holy Spirit is a person and that He is God, and not just God's active impersonal force and power.

The Jehovah's Witnesses' Teaching Concerning the Holy Spirit

Jehovah's Witnesses teach concerning the Holy Spirit that:

". . . The holy spirit is the invisible active force of the Almighty God that moves his servants to do his will" (Let God Be True, 2nd Edition, p. 108).

As for the 'Holy Spirit,' the so-called 'third Person of the Trinity,' we have already seen that it is not a person, but God's active force (The Truth That Leads To Eternal Life, Brooklyn: Watchtower Bible and Tract Society, 1968, p. 24).

Evangelical Christianity's Teaching Concerning the Holy Spirit

Evangelical Christianity believes and teaches that the Holy Spirit is a person and the third person of the Trinity. The qualities of personality consist of mind, will and emotions and all three of these qualities are given to the Holy Spirit.

Mind — Romans 8:27
Will — I Corinthians 12:11
Emotions — Ephesians 4:30

Further evidence that the Holy Spirit is a person and is God is seen in Acts 5:1-11. Peter said that Ananias had lied to the Holy Spirit in verses 3 and 4 and that he had not lied to men, but to God. When Ananias lied to the Holy Spirit, he lied to God.

The following verses teach that the Holy Spirit will teach, guide, speak, convict, witness, comfort, glorify, etc. All of these are qualities of personality.

Scripture   Key Verses

John 14:16-26 .... vs. 26
John 15:18-27 .... vs. 26
John 16:1-15 .... vs. 14

Acts 5:1-6 .... vs. 3-4
Acts 13:1-3 .... vs. 2
Acts 16:6-10 .... vs. 6-7
Acts 20:17-35 .... vs. 23
Acts 21:7-14 .... vs. 11
Romans 8:1-27 .... vs. 14,16, 26-27
I Corinthians 2:6-16 .... vs. 10-11
I Corinthians 12:1-3, 12-13 .... vs. 3, 13
Galatians 5:16-25 .... vs. 22
Ephesians 1:3-14 .... vs. 13-14
Ephesians 4:25-32 .... vs. 30
Titus 3:1-7 .... vs. 5
Hebrews 10:26-31 .... vs. 29
Jude 1:17-23 .... vs. 20
Revelation 22:17 .... vs. 17

The following verses show some of the Holy Spirit's activity in the Old Testament.

1. In creation of the earth — Genesis 1:1-2
2. In creation of angels — Psalms 33:6
3. In creation of man — Job 33:4
4. In preserving creation —Psalms 104:29-30
5. In empowering for service — Judges 6:34
6. In giving wisdom for leadership — Numbers 27:18
7. In empowering for strength — Judges 13:25; 14:6,19; 15:14

III. THE TRINITY

You must show them Scripturally that there is one God in three persons: The Father, the Son and the Holy Spirit; that all three persons are God and not just one God in one person named Jehovah.

The Jehovah's Witnesses' Teaching
Concerning the Trinity

Jehovah's Witnesses teach concerning the Trinity that:

> The doctrine, in brief, is that there are three gods in one: 'God the Father, God the Son, and God the Holy Ghost,' all three equal in power, substance and eternity (Let God Be True, Brooklyn: Watchtower Bible and Tract Society, 2nd Edition, p. 100).

> The obvious conclusion is, therefore, that Satan is the originator of the trinity doctrine (Ibid., p. 101).

> The trinity doctrine was not conceived by Jesus or the early Christians (Ibid., p. 111).

Evangelical Christianity's Teaching
Conerning the Trinity

The Baptist Faith and Message, which is a confessional statement adopted by the Southern Baptist Convention on May 9, 1963, expresses this doctrine clearly when it states:

> There is one and only one living and true God. He is an intelligent, spiritual, and personal Being, the Creator, Redeemer, Preserver, and Ruler of the universe. God is infinite in holiness and all other perfections. To Him we owe the highest love, reverence, and obedience. The eternal God reveals Himself to us as Father,

Son, and Holy Spirit, with distinct personal attributes, but without division of nature, essence, or being.

This confession stresses both the oneness of God and His threefold revelation of the persons within the one God. One God in three persons: Father, Son and Holy Spirit is the evangelical statement of the Trinity.

Scriptures to Be Used
Concerning the Trinity

Scripture	Key Verses
Matthew 3:13-17	vs. 16, 17
Matthew 28:16-20	vs. 19
Luke 1:26-38	vs. 35
John 15:18-27	vs. 26
Acts 5:17-32	vs. 29-32
Romans 8:26-39	vs. 27, 31, 34
I Corinthians 12:1-11	vs. 4-6
II Corinthians 13:11-14	vs. 14
Galatians 4:1-7	vs. 4, 6
Ephesians 1:3-14	vs. 3, 7, 13
Ephesians 2:11-22	vs. 18
Ephesians 4:1-6	vs. 4-6
II Thessalonians 2:13-15	vs. 13-14
Titus 3:1-7	vs. 4-6
I Peter 1:1-2	vs. 2
I John 5:1-13	vs. 4, 5, 7
Revelation 1:1-8	vs. 1, 4
Revelation 5:1-14	vs. 1, 6, 8
Revelation 22:1-21	vs. 1, 17

There is evidence in the Old Testament of the

triune nature of God although it is not as clear as it is in the New Testament after the incarnation of Christ and the outpouring of the Holy Spirit.

1. The triune nature of God in the Old Testament is seen through the emphasis put upon three persons: God or Lord, the Angel of the Lord and the Spirit of God.

> In the beginning <u>God</u> created the heavens and the earth.
> Genesis 1:1

> <u>The angel of the Lord</u> said to her further, 'Behold, you are with child, And you shall bear a son; And you shall call his name Ishmael, Because the Lord has given heed to your affliction.' Then she called the name of the Lord who spoke to her, "Thou art a God who sees"; for she said, 'Have I even remained alive here after seeing Him?'
> Genesis 16:11, 13

> <u>The Spirit of God</u> has made me, and the breath of the Almighty gives me life.
> Job 33:4

2. The angel of the Lord is distinguished from God, but is a special revelation and manifestation of God. He is one in name with God Himself and in power, in redemption and blessing, in worshipfulness and honor. He is called God in Genesis 16:13, the God of Bethel in Genesis 31:13, exchanges places with God or Lord in Genesis 28:13 and Exodus 3:4, and He bears the name of God within Him in Exodus 23:21. He redeems from all evil (Genesis 48:16), res-

cues Israel from the hand of the Egyptians (Exodus 3:8), cleaves the waters and dries up the sea (Exodus 14:21), preserves the people of God in the way, brings them safely into Canaan, causes them to triumph over their enemies (Exodus 3:8 and 23:20), is to be absolutely obeyed as though He were God Himself (Exodus 23:20-23) and always encamps around those who fear the Lord (Psalms 34:7 and 35:5) (Quoted from the book: Our Reasonable Faith by Herman Bavinck, p. 149).

3. Just as God carries out His redemptive activities through the angel of the Lord who is distinguished from God, but is a special manifestation of Him, so He by His Spirit gives out all kinds of energies and gifts to His people. In the Old Testament, the Spirit of the Lord is the source of all life and ability. He grants courage and strength to the judges, to Othniel (Judges 3:10), Gideon (Judges 6:34), Jephthah (Judges 11:29), and to Samson (Judges 14:6 and 15:14). He grants artistic perception to the makers of the priests garment, the tabernacle and the temple, and He gives wisdom and understanding to the judges who bear the burden of the people alongside of Moses (Numbers 11:17, 25). He gives the spirit of prophecy to the prophets and renewal and sanctification and guidance to all of God's children (Psalms 51:12-13 and 143:10) (Quoted from Our Reasonable Faith by Herman Bavinck, p. 149).

4. There are verses in the Old Testament which are trinitarian in their expression:

> The Lord bless you, and keep you;
> The Lord make His face shine on you,
> And be gracious to you;

The <u>Lord</u> lift up His countenance on you,
And give you peace.

> Numbers 6:24-26

And one called out to another and said, "<u>Holy,
Holy, Holy</u> is the Lord of hosts, the whole earth
is full of His glory."

> Isaiah 6:3

I shall make mention of the lovingkindness of
  <u>the Lord</u>, the praises of the Lord,
According to all that the Lord has granted us,
And the great goodness toward the house of Is
  rael,
Which He has granted them according to
  His compassion,
And according to the multitude of His lov-
  ingkindness.
For He said, Surely, they are my people, sons
  who will not deal falsely.
So He became their Savior.
In all of their affliction He was afflicted,
And <u>the angel of His presence saved them</u>;
In His love and in His mercy He redeemed them;
And He lifted them and carried them all the
  days of old.
But they rebelled
And grieved His <u>Holy Spirit</u>;
Therefore, He turned Himself to become their
  enemy,
He fought against them.
Then His people remembered the days of old, of
  Moses.
Where is He who brought them up out of the
  sea with the shepherds of His flock?
Where is He who put His Holy Spirit in the

midst of them.
Who caused His glorious arm to go at the right
    hand of Moses,
Who divided the waters before them to make for
    Himself an everlasting name,
Who led them through the depths?
Like the horse in the wilderness, they did not
    stumble;
As the cattle which go down into the valley,
The Spirit of the Lord gave them rest.
So didst Thou lead Thy people,
To make for Thyself a glorious name.

                        Isaiah 63:7-14

5. The Christian church down through the centuries has used Scriptural language to state the distinct relationship of the three persons in one God by expressing it as written in The Baptist Confession of Faith of 1689 that:

". . . the Father is of none, neither begotten nor proceeding; the Son is eternally begotten of the Father; the Holy Spirit proceeding from the Father and the Son; all infinite, without beginning, therefore but one God . . ."

6. The doctrine of the Trinity (the doctrine of one God in three persons) can be further explained as follows:

a. The Father alone has the quality of Fatherhood.
            Matthew 11:25-27
            John 17:1
            I Corinthians 8:6
            Ephesians 3:14-15
            II Peter 1:17

b. The Son alone has the quality of being begotten.

Psalms 2:7
John 1:14, 18
John 3:16, 18
John 16:27
I John 4:9

c. The Spirit alone has the quality of proceeding from both the Father and Son.

John 14:26
John 15:26
John 16:7, 13-16
Acts 16:6-7
Romans 8:9
Galatians 4:6

7. The New Testament emphasis on the three persons of the Trinity is understood in terms of <u>God/ Lord/Spirit</u>. God refers to the Father, Lord to the Son and Spirit to the Holy Spirit:

There is one body and one Spirit, just as also you were called in one hope of your calling; one Lord, one faith, one baptism, one God and Father of all who is over all and through all and in all.

Ephesians 4:4-6

The grace of the Lord Jesus Christ, and the love of God, and the fellowship of the Holy Spirit, be with you all.

II Corinthians 13:14

8. The emphasis upon the triune nature of God

is seen in that all things are from the Father, through the Son and in the Holy Spirit.

> Yet for us there is but one God, the Father, from whom are all things, and we exist for Him; and one Lord, Jesus Christ, through whom are all things, and we exist through Him.
> I Corinthians 8:6

> Or do you not know that your body is a temple of the Holy Spirit who is in you, whom you have from God, and that you are not your own?
> I Corinthians 6:19

9. The three persons of the Trinity are seen in our salvation as:

a. The Father	is over us	in electing grace
b. The Son	is for us	in redeeming grace
c. The Spirit	is in us	in regenerating grace

Within the triune nature of God's being the Father is first, the Son is second and the Spirit is third.

10. When witnessing to a Jehovah's Witness about the doctrine of the Trinity, the best way to express the Trinity is to explain how a lost person is saved:

a. God the Holy Spirit convicts the sinner of his need for a Savior:
   John 16:7-11

b. God the Son is the Lord and Savior that sinners must trust in order to be saved.
   John 3:16, 36

John 20:30-31
Romans 10:9-13

c. God the Father becomes their heavenly Father and they become His son through trusting the Lord Jesus Christ:
John 1:12-13
John 14:6
Galatians 4:4-7

11.   The triune nature of God is understood through the prayer life of a Christian:
a. We pray to God the Father.
Matthew 6:9
Ephesians 1:1-23
Ephesians 3:14-29

b. We pray through God the Son.
John 14:6
Romans 8:34
I Timothy 2:5

c. We pray as God the Spirit prays within us.
Romans 8:26-27

12.   The triune nature of one God in three persons is best summarized by Dr. Herman Bavinck in his book Our Reasonable Faith.

For the believers come to know the workings of the Father, the Creator of all things, He who gave them life, and breath, and all things. They learn to know Him as the Lawgiver who gave out His holy commandments in order that they should walk in them. They learn to know Him as the Judge who is provoked to terrible wrath

by all the unrighteousness of men and who in
no sense holds the guilty guiltless. And they
learn to know Him, finally, as the Father who
for Christ's sake is their God and Father, on
whom they trust so far that they do not doubt
but that He will supply for every need of body
and soul, and that He will convert all evil which
accrues to them in this vale of tears into good.
They know that He can do this as Almighty God
and that He wants to do it as a faithful Father.
Hence they confess: I believe in God, the Father,
the Almighty, Creator of heaven and earth.

Thus, too, they learn to know in themselves the
workings of the Son, He who is the only-begot-
ten of the Father, conceived in Mary of the Holy
Spirit. They learn to know Him as their highest
Prophet and Teacher, He who has perfectly revealed to them the secret counsel and will of
God in the matter of their redemption. They
learn to know Him as their only Highpriest, who
has redeemed them by the one sacrifice of His
body, and who still constantly intercedes for
them with the Father. They learn to know Him
as their eternal King, who rules them with His
Word and Spirit and who shelters and preserves
them in their redemption. Hence they confess: I
believe in Jesus Christ, God's only begotten
Son, our Lord.

And they also learn to recognize in themselves
the workings of the Holy Spirit, He who regener-
ates them and leads them into all truth. They
learn to know Him as the Operator of their faith,
He who through that faith causes them to share
in Christ and all His benefits. They learn to

know Him as the Comforter, He who prays in them with unutterable longings and who testifies with their spirit that they are children of God. They learn to know Him as the pledge of their eternal inheritance, He who preserves them until the day of their redemption. And they therefore confess: I believe also in the Holy Spirit.

Thus the confession of the trinity is the sum of the Christian religion. Without it neither the creation nor the redemption nor the sanctification can be purely maintained.
Every departure from this confession leads to error in other heads of doctrine, just as a mistaken representation of the articles of faith can be traced back to a misconception of the doctrine of the trinity. We can truly proclaim the mighty works of God only when we recognize and confess them as the one great work of Father, Son, and Spirit.

In the love of the Father, the grace of the Son and the fellowship of the Holy Spirit is contained the whole salvation of men (Quoted from Our Reasonable Faith by Herman Bavinck, pp. 160-161).

We have taken more time with the doctrine of the Trinity because this is the major stumbling block for Jehovah's Witnesses concerning Christianity. Once they see the truth of the doctrine of the Trinity (which is revealed only by the Holy Spirit), they can then trust Jesus Christ as the God-man and their Savior and Lord.

IV. THE RESURRECTION

You must show them Scripturally that Jesus Christ was raised from the dead with the same physical body He had before His crucifixion but that His body was raised incorruptible and glorified and not just as a spirit creature.

The Jehovah's Witnesses' Teaching Concerning the Resurrection

Jehovah's Witnesses teach concerning Christ's resurrection that:

". . . In His resurrection he was no more human. He was raised as a spirit creature . . ." (The Kingdom Is At Hand, p. 258).

". . . Jehovah God raised him from the dead, not as a human Son, but as a mighty immortal spirit Son . . . So the King Christ Jesus was put to death in the flesh and was resurrected an invisible spirit creature (Let God Be True, 2nd Edition, pp. 40, 138).

Therefore the bodies in which Jesus manifested himself to his disciples after his return to life were not the body in which he was nailed to the tree. They were merely materialized for the occasion, resembling on one or two occasions the body in which he died (The Kingdom Is At Hand, p. 259).

Evangelical Christianity's Teaching Concerning the Resurrection

Evangelical Christianity believes and teaches that the resurrection of Jesus Christ means that He arose physically from the dead in the same body in which He suffered but that it is now an incorruptible and glorified body.

Scriptures Which Teach the Bodily Resurrection of Jesus Christ

The following Scriptures reveal the bodily resurrection of our Lord and Savior Jesus Christ.

Scripture   Key Verses

Matthew 16:21-23 .... vs. 21
Matthew 17:22-23 .... vs. 23
Matthew 20:17-19 .... vs. 19
Matthew 27:45-56 .... vs. 53
Matthew 28:1-20 .... vs. 6, 9
Mark 16:1-8 .... vs. 6
Luke 24:1-12 .... vs. 3, 7
Luke 24:36-49 .... vs. 37,39,40, 46
John 2:13-22 .... vs. 19-22
John 20:1-10 .... vs. 9
John 20:19-23 .... vs. 20
John 20:24-29 .... vs. 25, 27
Acts 1:1-5 .... vs. 3
Acts 2:22-36 .... vs. 24, 32
Acts 5:29-32 .... vs. 30
Acts 10:34-43 .... vs. 40, 41
Acts 13:16-41 .... vs. 30,33,34, 37
Acts 17:22-31 .... vs. 31
Romans 1:1-4 .... vs. 4

Refuting the Jehovah's Witnesses' Use of I Corinthians 15:45 and I Peter 3:18

There are two verses of Scripture the Jehovah's Witnesses always mention to prove their teaching: I Corinthians 15:45 and I Peter 3:18.

I Corinthians 15:45
"So it is written: The first man Adam became a living being, the last Adam a life-giving spirit."
New International Version

This verse means that Christ after His resurrection has become the Giver of Life. He gives this life through the person of the Holy Spirit.

I Peter 3:18
"For Christ died for sins once for all, the righteous for the unrighteous, to bring you to God. He was put to death

in the body but made alive by the
Spirit."

New International Version

This verse means that God raised Jesus physically
from the dead by the power of the Holy Spirit. The
Apostle Paul wrote this same truth in Romans 8:11,
"And if the Spirit of Him who raised Jesus from the
dead is living in you, He who raised Christ from the
dead will also give life to your mortal bodies through
His Spirit, who lives in you."

The main point to emphasize is that I Corinthians 15:45 and I Peter 3:18 in no way contradict the
many clear passages which teach the physical resurrection of our Lord. There are so many clear passages that teach Christ's resurrection from the dead
physically that these two verses cannot be used to
deny or disprove this truth.

V. SALVATION

You must show them Scripturally that man is
saved by pure grace through repentance toward God
and faith in the Lord Jesus Christ and not on the
basis of any human merit or good works of any kind.

The Jehovah's Witnesses' Teaching Concerning Salvation

Jehovah's Witnesses teach concerning salvation
that:

Immortality is a reward for faithfulness. It does
not come automatically to a human at birth (Let
God Be True, 2nd Edition, p. 74).

Those people of good will today who avail themselves of the provision and who steadfastly abide in this confidence will find Christ Jesus to be their "everlasting Father" (Isaiah 9:6) (Ibid., p. 121).

We have learned that a person could fall away and be judged unfavorably either now or at Armageddon, or during the thousand years of Christ's reign, or at the end of the final test . . . into everlasting destruction (From Paradise Lost To Paradise Regained, p. 241).

Evangelical Christianity's Teaching Concerning Salvation

Christianity clearly teaches that salvation is a gift of God received by God's grace through repentance and faith in Jesus Christ as Lord and Savior.

The Baptist Faith and Message says concerning salvation: "Repentance and faith are inseparable experiences of grace. Repentance is a genuine turning from sin toward God. Faith is the acceptance of Jesus Christ and commitment of the entire personality to Him as Lord and Savior."

Scriptures to Use Concerning Salvation

Scripture   Key Verses

Matthew 3:1-12 .... vs. 2, 8, 11
Matthew 4:12-17 .... vs. 17
Luke 13:1-9 .... vs. 3, 5
Luke 24:44-49 .... vs. 47
John 1:9-13 .... vs. 12

John 3:1-21 .... vs. 16
John 3:31-36 .... vs. 36
John 7:37-39 .... vs. 38
John 11:17-29 .... vs. 25-26
John 20:30-31 .... vs. 31
Acts 3:11-26 .... vs. 19
Acts 11:1-18 .... vs. 17
Acts 13:13-41 .... vs. 38-39
Acts 15:1-11 .... vs. 11
Acts 16:16-34 .... vs. 30-31
Acts 17:22-31 .... vs. 30-31
Acts 20:17-35 .... vs. 21
Romans 1:16-17 .... vs. 16
Romans 3:19-30 .... vs. 22, 25
Romans 4:1-16 .... vs. 3, 5, 16
Romans 5:1 .... vs. 1
Romans 10:1-13 .... vs. 9-11
I Corinthians 15:1-4................ vs. 2
II Corinthians 7:8-10 .... vs. 9-10
Galatians 2:11-21 .... vs. 16
Galatians 3:1-14 .... vs. 6-9
Galatians 3:23-29 .... vs. 24, 26
Ephesians 2:1-10 .... vs. 8-9
Philippians 3:1-10 .... vs. 9
II Timothy 2:14-26 .... vs. 25
II Timothy 3:10-17 .... vs. 15
Titus 3:1-7 .... vs. 5
II Peter 3:8-13 .... vs. 9
I John 5:1-13 .... vs. 1, 5, 13
Revelation 16:1-21 .... vs. 9, 11

Explaining James 2:14-26
to Jehovah's Witnesses

When talking with Jehovah's Witnesses about salvation by grace and not works, you must be prepared to explain James 2:14-26. The following explanation will be helpful. The Apostle Paul in the book of Romans and Galatians answers the question: "How are we saved?" Whereas James, in the book of James, is answering the question: "Proof that we are saved?"

APOSTLE PAUL	JAMES
QUESTION: "How are we saved?"	QUESTION: "Proof that we are saved?"
Romans 4:3 "And Abraham believed God, and it was reckoned to him as righteousness." (See also Genesis 15:6)	James 2:21 "Was not Abraham our father justified by works, when he offered up Isaac his son on the altar?" (See also Genesis 22:9, 10, 12, 16-18)
Galatians 3:6 "Even so Abraham believed God, and it was reckoned to him as righteousness." (See also Genesis 15:6)	James 2:23 "And Abraham believed God, and it was reckoned to him as righteousness." (See also Genesis 15:6)

Paul and James start from different places in the Scriptures. Since Paul is dealing with the question of how we are saved, he begins by quoting Genesis 15:6, which declares that it is through faith in God's promise in Jesus Christ we are saved, whereas, James is dealing with the question of proof that we are saved, so he begins with Genesis 22:9-10, 12, 16-18, which declares Abraham gave evidence of his faith by offering up his son Isaac.   Then James quotes Genesis 15:6 to show that Abraham was saved by grace through faith in God's promise but that his offering up Isaac proved that his faith was real. James is saying that true faith is never a dead faith but is always active in works of obedience.

The Baptist Confession of Faith of 1689 says concerning justification under sections 1 and 2:

> Those whom God effectually calleth, he also freely justifieth, not by infusing righteousness into them, but by pardoning their sins, and by accounting and accepting their persons as righteous; not for anything wrought in them, or done by them, but for Christ's sake alone; not by imputing faith itself, the act of believing, or any other evangelical obedience to them, as their righteousness; but by imputing Christ's active obedience unto the whole law, and passive obedience in his death for their whole and sole righteousness, they receiving and resting on him and his righteousness by faith, which faith they have not of themselves; it is the gift of God.

> Faith thus receiving and resting on Christ and his righteousness, is the alone instrument of justification; yet it is not alone in the person justified, but is ever accompanied with all other saving graces, and is no dead faith but worketh by love.

Salvation by grace through faith in Jesus Christ always produces good works in the one converted. Good works are the natural outflow of the redeemed life and what God prepared beforehand that we should walk in:

> For by grace you have been saved through faith; and that not of yourselves, it is the gift of God; not as a result of works, that no one should boast. For we are His workmanship, created in Christ Jesus for good works, which God prepared beforehand, that we should walk in them.
>
> Ephesians 2:8-10

VI. HEAVEN

You must show them Scripturally that everyone who is a Christian has the hope of going to heaven and not just 144,000 Jehovah's Witnesses.

The Jehovah's Witnesses' Teaching Concerning Heaven

Jehovah's Witnesses teach concerning heaven that:

> For over 1900 years there was a gathering together of the "little flock" of 144,000 Christians who will rule with Christ. Only a few of these are left on earth. Most are already ruling with Christ in heaven (You Can Live Forever, pp. 163-164).

> Who and how many are able to enter it [the Kingdom]? The Revelation limits to 144,000 the number that become a part of the Kingdom and stand on heavenly Mount Zion . . . (Let God Be True, 2nd Edition, p. 136).

> He [Christ] went to prepare a heavenly place for

his associate heirs, "Christ's body," for they too will be invisible spirit creatures (Let God Be True, 2nd Edition, p. 138).

Evangelical Christianity's Teaching Concerning Heaven

Christianity teaches that every person who trusts Jesus Christ as their Lord and Savior will go to heaven and be with Christ forever.

Scriptures to Use Concerning Heaven

Scripture	Key Verses
Matthew 6:19-24	vs. 20, 21
Matthew 8:5-13	vs. 11
Matthew 25:31-46	vs. 34
Luke 10:17-20	vs. 20
Luke 16:19-31	vs. 22
Luke 23:39-43	vs. 43
John 14:1-6	vs. 2-3
John 17:22-26	vs. 24
II Corinthians 5:1-10	vs. 1, 2, 8
II Corinthians 12:1-6	vs. 2, 4
Philippians 3:17-21	vs. 20-21
Colossians 1:1-8	vs. 5
I Thessalonians 4:13-18	vs. 16-18
Hebrews 11:8-16	vs. 10, 16
Hebrews 12:18-24	vs. 22-23
I Peter 1:3-5	vs. 4
II Peter 3:10-13	vs. 13
Revelation 2:1-7	vs. 7
Revelation 7:9-17	vs. 13-17
Revelation 21:1-8	vs. 2-3

Revelation 21:10-27 .... vs. 10, 22-27
Revelation 21:1-5 .... vs. 1, 3-5

All of these Scriptures are addressed to all of
the people of God and not just 144,000 of them.
These Scriptures give hope to any born-again believer
that his final destiny is heaven.

VII.   HELL

You must show them Scripturally that hell is a
real place of conscious eternal torment for the lost
sinner and not just the grave where a person totally
ceases to exist.

The Jehovah's Witnesses' Teaching
Concerning Hell

Jehovah's Witnesses teach concerning hell that:

". . . The Bible hell is mankind's common grave .
. ." (Let God Be True, 2nd Edition, p. 92).

It is so plain that the Bible hell is mankind's
common grave that even an honest little child
can understand it, but not the religious theolo-
gians (Ibid., p. 92).

Who is responsible for this God-defaming doctrine of a hell of torment? The promulgator of it
is Satan himself. His purpose in introducing it
has been to frighten the people away from
studying the Bible and to make them hate God
(Ibid., p. 98).

The doctrine of a burning hell where the wicked are tortured eternally after death cannot be true, mainly for four reasons: (1) Because it is wholly unscriptural; (2) it is unreasonable; (3) it is contrary to God's love; and (4) it is repugnant to justice (Ibid., p. 99).

Evangelical Christianity's Teaching Concerning Hell

Christianity teaches that hell is a reality and those who reject Jesus Christ as their Savior and Lord will spend an eternity in hell separated from God.

Scripture	Key Verses
Matthew 5:21-26	vs. 22
Matthew 5:27-32	vs. 29
Matthew 11:20-24	vs. 22-24
Matthew 13:47-50	vs. 49-50
Matthew 18:1-9	vs. 6, 8-9
Matthew 25:31-46	vs. 41, 46
Mark 9:38-50	vs. 43-44, 47-48
Luke 16:19-31	vs. 22-24, 26
John 3:31-36	vs. 36
II Thessalonians 1:3-12	vs. 9
Hebrews 10:26-31	vs. 27, 31
II Peter 2:1-22	vs. 4, 21
Revelation 14:9-12	vs. 10-11
Revelation 20:11-15	vs. 14-15

All of these Scriptures warn of the terrible judgment of those who refuse to trust Jesus Christ as their Lord and Savior and die in their sins. To say that these verses are not describing a real place of

Hebrews 10:26-31 .... vs. 27, 31
II Peter 2:1-22 .... vs. 4, 21
Revelation 14:9-12 .... vs. 10-11
Revelation 20:11-15 .... vs. 14-15

All of these Scriptures warn of the terrible judgment of those who refuse to trust Jesus Christ as their Lord and Savior and die in their sins. To say that these verses are not describing a real place of eternal conscious torment for sinners is to make mockery of language.

VIII.   SECOND COMING OF JESUS CHRIST

You must show them Scripturally that Jesus Christ will return visibly, bodily, and in glory with His angels to gather together His church, destroy the Antichrist and his evil government at the battle of Armageddon, and reign as King of Kings and Lord of Lords; and not that He returned invisibly in 1914 to rule His Kingdom until the battle of Armageddon which will destroy everyone but Jehovah's Witnesses.

The Jehovah's Witnesses' Teaching Concerning the Second Coming of Jesus Christ

Jehovah's Witnesses teach concerning the Second Coming of Christ that: Jesus Christ returned as an invisible spirit in 1914.

> Christ Jesus returns, not again as a human, but as a glorious spirit person (Let God Be True, 2nd Edition, p. 196).

". . . Christ Jesus came to the Kingdom in A.D. 1914, but unseen to men" (The Truth Shall Make You Free, p. 300).

Evangelical Christianity's Teaching Concerning the Second Coming of Jesus Christ

Christianity teaches that Christ will come again in glory and power to rule as King of Kings and Lord of Lords.

Scripture	Key Verses
Matthew 13:36-43	vs. 39-43
Matthew 16:21-28	vs. 27
Matthew 19:27-30	vs. 28
Matthew 24:1-31	vs. 29-31
Matthew 24:32-41	vs. 37, 39-41
Mark 13:1-27	vs. 24-27
Luke 17:22-37	vs. 34-35
Luke 21:5-28	vs. 25-28
Acts 1:6-11	vs. 11
I Corinthians 1:4-9	vs. 7-8
I Corinthians 15:20-28	vs. 23-28
I Thessalonians 1:2-10	vs. 10
I Thessalonians 4:13-18	vs. 16-18
II Thessalonians 1:3-12	vs. 7-10
II Thessalonians 2:1-12	vs. 3, 8
II Timothy 4:1-4	vs. 1
Titus 2:11-14	vs. 13
Hebrews 9:23-28	vs. 28
James 5:7-11	vs. 7
I Peter 5:1-5	vs. 4
II Peter 3:1-13	vs. 10-13
I John 3:1-3	vs. 2

II Thessalonians 1:3-12 .... vs. 7-10
II Thessalonians 2:1-12 .... vs. 3, 8
II Timothy 4:1-4 .... vs. 1
Titus 2:11-14 .... vs. 13
Hebrews 9:23-28 .... vs. 28
James 5:7-11 .... vs. 7
I Peter 5:1-5 .... vs. 4
II Peter 3:1-13 .... vs. 10-13
I John 3:1-3 .... vs. 2
Revelation 1:4-8 .... vs. 7
Revelation 14:14-20 .... vs. 14, 19-20
Revelation 16:1-21 .... vs. 16
Revelation 19:11-21 .... vs. 11, 19-21
Revelation 20:1-10 .... vs. 2, 4-10

All these Scriptures teach that Jesus Christ is going to return visibly, bodily, and in glory with His angels to rapture His church, destroy the Antichrist and his Kingdom of evil and reign as King of Kings and Lord of Lords. His coming will be visible to the whole world and come immediately after the "great tribulation" that is coming upon the world. Jesus Christ did not return in 1914, but He will return soon.

CHAPTER SIX

The Follow-up for a Converted
Jehovah's Witness

When you lead a Jehovah's Witness to Christ, you have a biblical responsibility to help nurture and strengthen his Christian growth. The mental and emotional pains of leaving the Watchtower organization require a tremendous amount of support and encouragement from the Christian community. He needs immediate follow-up by mature Christians in the body of Christ.

He must be instructed in the basic fundamentals of Christianity. Using the major doctrines and Scriptures given in this booklet is a good place to begin. Introduce him to the local church of which you are a member and encourage him to follow Christ in baptism. He needs to be a part of the main teaching organizations of the local church. Any good material on the new life in Christ should be shared with him. Much love, patience and personal encouragement must be given to a new convert.

Converted Jehovah's Witnesses will have numerous questions that need to be answered. Be prepared to answer their questions or have someone more mature and qualified to help them. Good reading material and tapes are extremely valuable in helping a converted Jehovah's Witness in his Christian growth. They make aggressive and dedicated Christians and with the right follow-up, their spiritual growth and maturity in grace and knowledge of Jesus Christ is usually very rapid.

CONCLUSION

This booklet has been written with the intended purpose of helping Christians to share their faith with Jehovah's Witnesses with the goal of leading them to the saving knowledge of Jesus Christ. There is a lot of material in this booklet and although it is not necessary to be able to know every Scripture that is listed before one can be effective in leading them to Christ, it does take a good grasp of the main doctrinal truths with Scriptural support to refute the Jehovah's Witnesses error and to lead them to Christ.

The more one studies each point and commits a number of Scriptures to memory, the better equipped he will be to confront Jehovah's Witnesses with the truth. One should begin with the skeletal outline in Chapter Four and then add to these other Scriptures as found in Chapter Five. With this knowledge, faithful prayer and the filling of God's Holy Spirit, you will be fully prepared to witness to a Jehovah's Witness. May God grant you much fruit in sharing Christ with Jehovah's Witnesses.

So faith comes from hearing, and hearing by the word of Christ.
Romans 10:17

Trinity

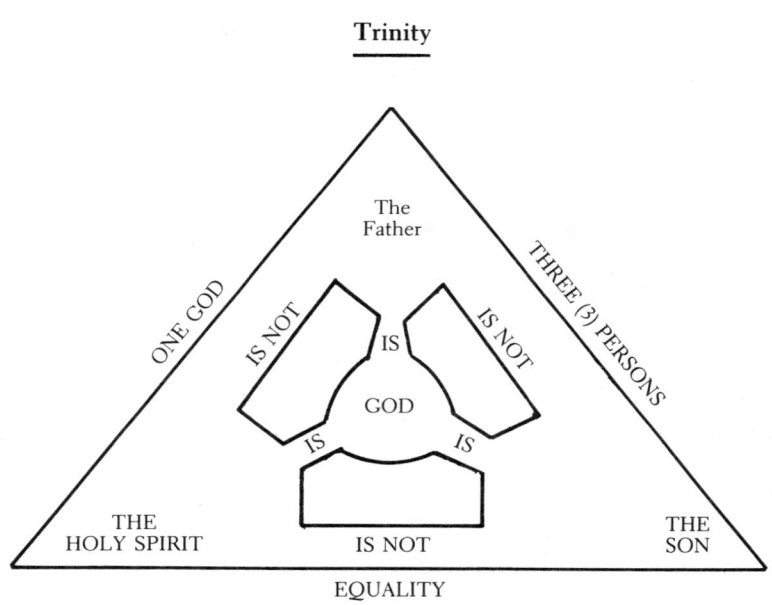

BIBLIOGRAPHY

Bavinck, Herman. Our Responsible Faith. Baker House Publishers, 1956.

Martin, Walter. The Kingdom of the Cults. Bethany House Publishers, 1985.

— — — — —. Jehovah's Witnesses. Bethany House Publishers, 1957.

McDowell, Josh and Stewart, Don. Understanding the Cults. Here's Life Publishers, Inc., 1982.

Van Baalen, Jan. The Chaos of the Cults. Wm. B. Eerdman's Publishers, 1962.

The Baptist Confession of Faith of 1689.

The Baptist Faith and Message. Adopted by the Southern Baptist Convention, May 8, 1963.

You Can Live Forever In Paradise On Earth. Watch Tower Bible and Tract Society of Pennsylvania. 1982.